Contents

The Earth we live in

What is the Universe made of?

Energy, light and gravity

Big Bang Theory

The Universe

Badri Seshadri

The Universe
Badri Seshadri ©

First Edition: December 2007
80 Pages
Printed in India.

ISBN 978-81-8368-617-4
Pro-ya-en - 1

Prodigy Books
177/103, First Floor,
Ambal's Building, Lloyds Road,
Royapettah, Chennai 600 014.
Ph: +91-44-4200-9603

Email : support@nhm.in
Website : www.nhm.in

The Earth we live in

Hello friends! Today let's talk about the universe of which we are all part of—the bright, warm Sun, our beautiful planet Earth, the twinkling stars, the huge wispy clouds, the heavenly moon and more. Who created all these? Let's find out…

We are quite familiar with the Earth we live in. All of us say that our Earth is spherical in shape. Today, we know a lot about the Earth we live in. But our ancestors who lived a few centuries ago had very different ideas about our Earth.

Just a few centuries ago, humans thought the Earth was flat, as flat as your dosa. They thought the flat Earth was bound on the edges by the vast ocean. If you travelled across the oceans, you could fall off the edge into an abyss—a bottomless underworld. They also thought the

Earth was made of several layers. As you dug deeper into the Earth, they expected you to come across those layers and such regions were considered to be occupied by demons and other scary creatures.

Likewise, they thought there was a layer of sky placed firmly above the Earth. And angels and gods were supposed to live high in the sky.

With such a layered, flat Earth, our ancestors could not clearly explain how the Sun rose in the east and set in the west and how again, the next day, the Sun rose in the east. Nor could they explain the Moon and the stars.

These phenomena were seen as the handiwork of angels and gods. So was the mysterious occurrence of rain. Unlike the appearing and disappearing of the Sun and the Moon, which happened at periodic and regular intervals, the rains were somewhat irregular.

Our ancestors were exposed to well defined seasons—summer, winter, autumn and spring. This too was quite regular and repeated once a year. Our ancestors did travel quite a bit to fight their wars and to trade in goods.

During these travels, they observed that the seasons varied quite a bit. They had never seen snow in some places, but elsewhere snow and ice were common. It was just unbearably hot in some places, but very pleasant to live elsewhere.

All these changes were quite difficult to explain.

From Flat Earth to Spherical Earth

It is quite possible that at least some of the folks in the past knew that the Earth was spherical. If people could see the Sun and the Moon and found them to be round, it was not impossible to guess that the Earth could be spherical too.

The Greeks had guessed that the Earth was spherical. But from the 4th century AD, the common European thinking was that the Earth was flat. This idea persisted for a long time—in fact several centuries.

In India, the earliest Dasavatara story—Matsyavatara—saw the Earth as a flat, thin layer. The demons could easily roll the flat Earth like the way you roll your bed, take the rolled Earth under the oceans and hide it. It took Mahavishnu in the form of a fish to go under the sea and fight the demons and recover the rolled-up Earth.

If our ancestors had looked at the approaching ships at sea, they could have guessed that the Earth's top surface was curved. We get to see the masthead appearing first and only much later the hull of the ship.

With this evidence, all we can guess is that the surface of the Earth is like an inverted bowl–a dome. To really prove that the Earth is a sphere, you had to travel around the Earth in a circular path and come back to the same place from where you started.

This was indeed done by **Ferdinand Magellan**, a Portuguese explorer. In those days various European countries financed shipping expeditions to find new routes to India. The Europeans were buying spices from India and this trade happened through the land route via Arabia and Venice. The Europeans wanted a sea route which they could control directly, rather than pay a heavy commission to Arabian and Venetian traders.

The explorers went in large ships searching for new routes. That is how they ended up discovering what they called new worlds such as North America and South America.

There were two key tools a sea voyaging explorer was in need of. The first was a compass and the second, a reliable map. A compass is an instrument that has a magnetic needle enclosed in a glass case.

A magnet has a peculiar property. When a magnetic needle is allowed to turn freely on its axis, it will always align itself along a North Pole to South Pole direction. This is because the Earth itself is a giant magnet. Any other magnet will try to align itself along the Earth's magnetic axis, i.e., north to south. Thus, a compass will show the direction the holder of the compass is travelling in, with respect to the North Pole-South Pole axis.

The earliest compasses were made by the Chinese in the 11th century AD, while Europeans made them in the 13th century AD. It was only after this invention that explorers could boldly venture into the sea.

The second tool was the map. The method of making maps is called cartography. Maps have been in use since several thousand years. Just that older maps were not exact. But modern maps were created by surveying the land using tools such as compass and sextant (which measures angles accurately).

A map is the drawing of the boundaries of a land area bordered by oceans. Take any point as a reference. From this point, measure the distance to the seashore. By gradually shifting the angles from this point, the respective lengths to the seashore are measured, along with the respective angles. A miniature version of the land surveyed can be drawn on a piece of paper by geometrically scaling the distances (miles to inches).

Further, geometric corrections are required in projecting an area on a spherical surface to a flat sheet of paper. This technique was known as early as the 2nd century AD. It was developed by the scientist **Ptolemy**.

Mapmaking reached great heights between the 13th and 15th centuries AD. It became even better after this period, with the help of telescopes.

Armed with maps and compass, Magellan successfully circumnavigated–that is, went around–the Earth. He left on 10 August 1519 from the Spanish coast. Along the way, he died in a battle on 17 April 1521. But his sailors continued the voyage and arrived back in Spain on 6 September 1522.

After this trip, no one doubted that the Earth was anything other than spherical.

Which goes around what?

It was easy to project thereafter that almost all celestial bodies such as the Sun, the Moon and the Earth were spherical in shape. It was also easy to observe that they were travelling in some sort of a circular path.

However, the question was, which was going around what?

It was believed in Europe that Earth being the place God chose for human beings to live in-surely it must be at the centre. The Sun and the Moon, then must be going around the Earth in circles. That could describe day and night perfectly.

Several ancient cultures had guessed that the Sun could be at the centre, with the Earth and several other planets going around the Sun in circles. In India, the astronomer Aryabhatta, said around 500 AD that the Sun was at the centre, with the Earth going around the Sun. Aryabhatta perhaps also realised that the Earth was spherical.

But, in Europe, the Earth was seen to be at the centre. This view had its origins in Aristotle, the great Greek philosopher.

Even before Magellan started on his trip around the Earth, in the year 1514, **Nicolaus Copernicus**, an astronomer who was born in what is now Poland, came up with his theory of the Sun being the centre. This theory is known as the heliocentric theory. Helios means the Sun.

Copernicus wrote a book explaining his theory. He died in 1543, before his book was published.

In the meantime, there were significant advances in optics. Lenses were developed by grinding pieces of glass. A lens magnifies an object nearby several-fold. It also helps to see a faraway object, not normally seen by the naked eye.

Using lenses, instruments called telescopes were built. The telescopes were used to see objects in the sky. Now humans could clearly see several other celestial objects besides the Moon and also track their motion.

An Italian astronomer called **Galileo Galilei** built a large telescope and started observing celestial movements. Galileo could see as far as Jupiter and could observe several moons going around Jupiter.

If some object could circle another planet and not the Earth, why should we assume that everything is going around the Earth?

This prompted Galileo to agree with the Copernicus model.

When this theory became popular, the Christian Church felt uncomfortable. They were of the opinion that a theory that promoted the Sun as the centre was against their religion. They ordered Galileo to stop spreading his theories.

In 1633, the church banned his book, asked him to agree that he was wrong about the heliocentric theory and also got him arrested. He was then kept under house arrest, though not sent to jail.

Galileo spent the rest of his life confined to his house till his death in 1642.

In the end, Galileo won. Over the next century, scientists and thinkers slowly moved away from an Earth-centric theory to a Sun-centric theory and the church eventually gave in.

The Solar System

Ancient people spotted and discovered several planets which were close enough to the Earth. These planets were Mercury, Venus, Mars, Jupiter and Saturn. Until 1781, no other planet was discovered. So Galileo and other astronomers did not know of any other planet.

Armed with powerful telescopes, astronomers could now measure and track these five planets, along with our own dwelling place, Earth, and calculate their paths around the Sun.

It was only in 1781 that Sir William Herschel located Uranus, the seventh planet, using a telescope. This was the first planet to be discovered using a telescope. Soon, astronomers started looking around for other planets. But they were not very lucky. Neptune, the eighth planet was discovered only in 1846.

Galileo had observed Neptune using his telescope in 1612 and 1613. But he did not identify it as a planet and instead assumed that it was a star.

In 1930, another 'planet' was discovered and named Pluto. Much later, in 2006, scientists concluded that Pluto is not actually a planet. It is now considered to be merely a large piece of rock in a region called the Kuiper belt, a region beyond the eighth planet Neptune, which contains a large number of particles.

Understanding celestial motions

Let us now go back to the time of Galileo. **Johannes Kepler** was a German astronomer of that period.

All the astronomers before Kepler believed that celestial motion always happened in perfectly circular orbits. Whether it was the planets going around the Sun, or the Moon going around the Earth, the path was considered to be an exact circle.

Kepler however calculated and found that the path was, in almost all cases, an ellipse. An ellipse is an elongated circle. Even Galileo thought that Kepler was wrong. But Kepler was eventually proved right.

Some Indian astronomers before Kepler's time had also worked out that celestial paths were elliptic and used the idea in their calculations.

Kepler, through his observations and calculations, came up with the following conclusions:

1. The path of every planet is an ellipse, with the Sun as the focus of the ellipse. (See the accompanying picture.)

2. When the planet is closer to the Sun, it travels faster. When it is far away from the Sun, it travels slower.

With Kepler's theories and calculations, the only missing piece was a firm mathematical model.

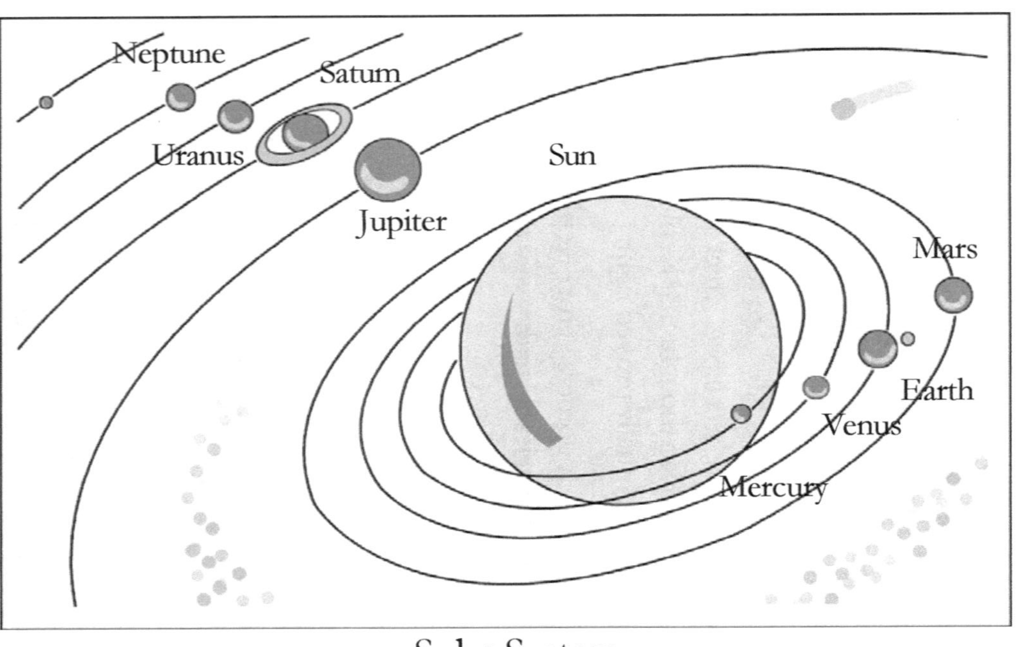

Neptune
Satum
Uranus
Jupiter
Sun
Mars
Earth
Venus
Mercury
Solar System

A mathematical framework

Kepler's ideas helped another great scientist, possibly the greatest ever, **Sir Isaac Newton**, to arrive at a complete mathematical model for celestial motions.

Isaac Newton lived between 1643 and 1727. Within this period, he built much of modern science and mathematics. He developed several mathematical tools, most notably differential and integral calculus. Using these tools, he provided the mathematical framework for celestial motion.

Newton was instrumental in explaining the most basic question—why one heavy body goes around another much heavier body?

Newton came up with his laws of motion, explained the concept of gravity, and completely described the motion of celestial bodies driven by gravity.

Gravity is a kind of force field created by any massive body in its vicinity. It is very similar to the magnetic force field created by a magnet. When you bring a small piece of iron near a magnet, the magnetic force field surrounding the magnet pulls the iron piece closer to the magnet.

Similarly, the gravitational force field surrounding a large mass attracts all the objects that come in its wake.

This is why any stone thrown up in the air, falls down on the surface of the Earth. This force attracts all bodies towards the centre of the Earth. It is the hardness of the surface of the Earth that is preventing us from being pulled to the core of the Earth.

Gravitational attraction depends on the mass of a large body and its radius. Thus, using Newton's theories, we can calculate the gravity on the surfaces of the Earth, the Moon and the Sun.

The gravitational force between the Earth and the Moon forces the smaller body to keep circling the larger body. This is the same reason why all the planets go around the Sun.

Thus, starting from Copernicus and ending with Newton, the theoretical framework for understanding celestial motion was put in place perfectly.

Measuring astronomical dimensions

How will you calculate the radius of the Earth? That is not too difficult. In fact, the earliest known estimate of the Earth's radius is from the 3rd century BC by a Greek mathematician **Eratosthenes**. (It is amazing that, even after this, most of Europe thought–for centuries–that the Earth was flat!)

The Earth rotates on its own axis, which runs through the poles, and then circles around the Sun. On certain days–known as solstice–the Sun stands exactly above a certain spot on the surface of the Earth. At noon, anywhere in this ring, there will not be any shadow cast on the ground. This happens twice a year, once over what is known as the Tropic of Cancer (an imaginary circle, at a certain distance from the equator), and once over the Tropic of Capricorn.

The Tropic of Cancer and Tropic of Capricorn are on either side of the equator, at equidistance from the equator.

Eratosthenes chose the summer solstice. On that day, at a location called Syene, there was no shadow at noon time, as that place was on the Tropic of Cancer. He measured the angle the shadow was making in Alexandria. Then, using the distance between Syene and Alexandria and the angle of the shadow, using geometry, Eratosthenes could measure the curvature of the Earth and its approximate radius.

To measure the distance between the Earth and the Sun, you need to monitor the motion of a nearby planet (say Venus) with respect to the Earth and the Sun. Since both Venus and Earth go around the Sun, one can measure the maximum angle caused by the line connecting Venus and Earth to the line connecting the Earth and the Sun.

This will help us determine the distance between the Earth and the Sun as a function of the distance between the Earth and Venus. Thus, astronomers were able to express any inter-planetary distance as a function of the Earth-Sun distance. We now need to know at least one distance to calculate all the other distances.

Using modern radars the distance between Venus and the Earth can be estimated accurately. However, a few centuries ago, before the invention of radar, the Earth-Sun distance was estimated by **Cassini**.

In 1672, Cassini had a friend go to a different place. They both simultaneously measured the position of Mars (another nearby planet) from these two places with respect to far away stars.

Based on this parallax (the difference in the observed positions of Mars) and the distance between the places they used for these measurements, they could calculate the distance between Mars and the Earth. Once this distance was known, all other distances popped out of the formulae already determined.

This gave a figure of the Earth-Sun distance to roughly 150 million kilometres.

Distance between the sun and the plants

Plants	Distance (Million km)
Mercury	57.91
Venus	108.2
Earth	149.6
Mars	227.94
Jupiter	778.33
Saturn	1,426.94
Uranus	2,870.99
Neptune	4,497.07

Measuring the mass of stars and planets

Astronomers were fully capable of measuring various distances. But measuring the mass of the Earth was more difficult. Not even Newton could do this, though he had developed all the necessary theories for calculating the mass of the Earth.

Newton had proposed that the gravitational force between two massive bodies directly depended on the masses of those two bodies and inversely depended on the square of the distance between them.

Henry Cavendish, another English physicist, born after Newton's death used Newton's theories and calculated the mass of the Earth accurately.

Thereafter, physicists used several similar methods to estimate the mass of all the planets, their moons and even the mass of the Sun.

The Solar System

With all the calculations of distance and mass, we now have the following understanding of the planetary system we are living in.

- The Sun is at the centre of our planetary system and it is a Star.

- We live on the surface of a sphere called the Earth which goes around the Sun in an elliptical orbit.

- The Earth also rotates about itself on its own axis.

- In addition to the Earth, there are seven other planets that orbit our Sun. The eight planets in the order of closeness to the Sun are: Mercury, Venus, Earth, Mars, Jupiter, Saturn, Uranus and Neptune.

- There are several other pieces flying around the Sun beyond Neptune in a region known as the Kuiper belt. The largest piece in that area is called Pluto, and for a long time we believed it to be the ninth planet.

- Several planets have one or more moons circling around them. Our Earth has one moon. But a few other planets have several moons. Saturn has a ring like structure around it.

- We know the mass and radius of all these planets, their moons, and for the Sun as well.

Having known all this, it was possible for us to explain pretty much whatever was happening in our own planet, the Earth.

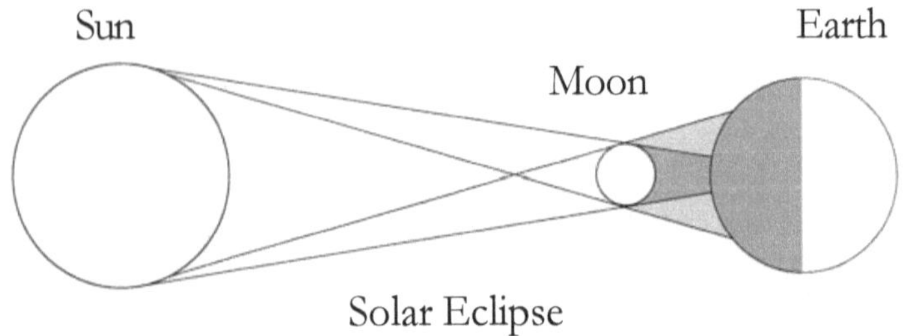

Solar Eclipse

Our planet is unique in that so far, we have found living beings only here. We have been lucky because we are at the ideal distance from the Sun. The Sun is a very hot sphere and heat and light radiate from it. The closest planet, Mercury, is just too hot to support any kind of life. The farther planets are too cold.

Water, which is extremely essential for living beings to survive, seems to be available only in our planet. A

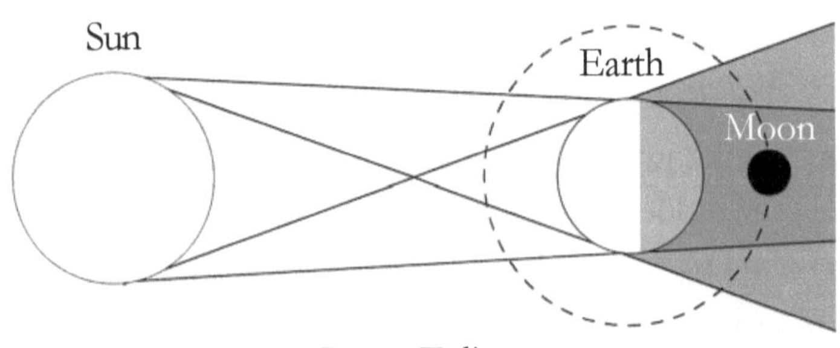

Lunar Eclipse

protective shield called the atmosphere containing air exists around our Earth and saves us from harmful solar radiation.

Oxygen, a vital ingredient for all living things, seems to be available only in our Earth's atmosphere.

Explaining the seasons

For too long our ancestors observed and noted down several events happening around us, without being able to explain all of them correctly. But with the theoretical base and understanding of the Solar System, it was possible to explain all these events. By early 20th century, almost all natural events happening on the Earth could be explained.

Day and night, the phases of the Moon including new moon day and full moon day, and partial moon sightings during the rest of the period, eclipses, solstices, equinoxes, tides in the ocean, rains, seasons, monsoons and cyclones— all of them could be explained by way of science.

All these physical phenomena were perfectly explainable scientific events caused by the Sun, motion of the planets and their moons, gravitational forces between various large bodies, heat and cold, evaporation, condensation, changes in air pressure in pockets and so on.

Explaining eclipses

One of the mysteries of our Earth was that on certain days, the bright Sun suddenly vanished for a brief period, as if someone came and swallowed it. On certain other days, in the night sky, the Moon vanished for a brief period (not merely going behind the clouds but completely out of sight) and then emerged.

They were known as the Solar Eclipse or Lunar Eclipse depending on which celestial body vanished.

According to Hindu mythology, demons ate the Sun and the Moon during these 'eclipse' times.

With scientific understanding of the motion of the Earth around the Sun and the motion of the Moon around the Earth, we can neatly explain the eclipses.

When the Moon comes in between the Sun and the Earth, for a brief period, people in a small area on the Earth's surface will not be able to see the Sun. This is the solar eclipse.

The Moon does not have a light source of its own. It can only be seen when the light from the Sun reflects on the Moon. If the Sun, the Earth and the Moon are all in a straight line, with the Moon getting caught in the shadow of the Earth, it will be completely hidden. As the Moon moves out of the shadow of the Earth, it picks up the light from the Sun and is visible once again. This is the lunar eclipse.

Knowing our boundaries

Even after the discoveries of other planets and the Sun, we still had a lot more to discover.

There were several twinkling stars in the sky, seen only at night time. During the day, the bright sunlight dispersed through the atmosphere prevented us from seeing these stars.

The field of astronomy had now to contend with these millions of stars. How far are they from us? How heavy are they? What are they?

Radio telescopes

The optical telescopes had reached their limits.

Through advances in physics, it was learnt that visible light—the white light from the Sun and other sources—was only a part of what could be called 'light'. Light was more generally defined as electromagnetic radiation. These light waves had different frequencies. Depending upon their frequencies, the human eyes could either see them, or not.

Beyond the visible light range, on either side of the spectrum lie ultra-violet rays, infra-red rays, X-rays, microwave radiation, gamma rays, radio waves used by our radio stations and so on. Technically all these waves can be called light. Of this, our eyes can only see a part, which is what is known as visible light.

This is similar to the sound wave spectrum. Our human ears can only hear sound within a specific frequency range. However dogs and other animals can hear sound at lower frequencies that we cannot hear. Bats can recognise ultrasound through their antennae. Some animals can see light of a frequency not seen by human eyes.

It is possible to build a telescope-like electronic device which can receive electromagnetic waves which are not in the visible range. Such telescopes are called radio telescopes. They consist of large dish antennas similar to those we had before the days of direct-to-home satellite television.

These radio telescopes required electronic circuitry and were built only after the 1930s.

They were used to track signals coming from faraway locations. Like visible light from some stars, several other stars were sending electromagnetic radiation invisible to our eyes.

What are stars?

Stars are large bodies of matter known as plasma. We will try to understand more about this in the next chapter. Let us just assume for now that at the core of the star, there is a violent reaction going on which generates lots of heat and radiation.

The star closest to us is the Sun. It generates lots of heat, visible light and invisible radiation.

Using radio telescopes, scientists found astonishing things. Our Sun was not alone! The Universe consisted of several thousand, possibly millions of stars just as big as our Sun, and several that are much bigger than our Sun!

These stars are grouped together in formations known as galaxies. Our Sun and its planets and moons are part of what is known as the Milky Way galaxy. There are several Suns and planetary systems within this galaxy. And then, there are several galaxies.

These other galaxies and stars are far, far away. Light (visible or invisible–it does not matter) is known to have the highest velocity. It is supposed to travel at the rate of about 300,000 kilometres per second. Some of these stars are so far away, the light triggered from them now will reach us only after many years! By the time their light reaches us, those stars may have completely vanished!

Using this, a new measure for distance has been created. It is applied to astronomical distances called a 'light year'. A light year is the distance covered by light over a period of one year (365 days). We know that light travels at the speed of 300,000 kilometres every second. In one year, light would have travelled approximately 9,500,000,000,000 kilometres (9.5 trillion km).

Light from the Sun takes a mere 8.31 minutes to reach the Earth. But if you take the centre of our galaxy Milky Way, and measure the distance between this point and the centre point of the Sun, the distance will be 26,000 light years! (Now calculate this distance in kilometres!)

That is, even if you travel at the speed of light from the centre of the Sun, it will take you 26,000 years to reach the centre of our galaxy! If you have to travel to another galaxy, imagine how many more years it will take you!

Radio telescopes gave a view of how large our Universe was.

It was **Edwin Hubble**, an American astronomer, who discovered that there was more to this Universe than our own Milky Way galaxy. He pointed out that there were other galaxies such as the Andromeda galaxy, well outside the Milky Way galaxy.

In the meantime, several astronomers found data from distant stars a little puzzling. To understand this, let us take up a simple example. Stand near an approaching train. When the train comes closer to you, its whistling sound is at a higher pitch than when it is stationary. Similarly, when the train moves away from you, the sound is of a lower pitch.

This is called Doppler Effect. The same thing is applicable to electromagnetic waves as well.

The visible light is composed of seven colours. We see them in a rainbow. They are Violet, Indigo, Blue, Green, Yellow, Orange and Red. Violet is a high frequency light. Red is a low frequency light.

When a source emitting light moves away from us, we will see the light emitted from it as a shade of red. If the same light emitting source moves towards us, we will see the light as a shade of violet.

Astronomers found that faraway stars were emitting light shifting closer to red. This can only mean that faraway stars are moving away from us. Here 'us' means the Earth.

Hubble and others found another interesting thing. Both the stars closer to us and far away from us were shifting to red. But, the very distant stars were sending signals that were shifting much closer to red, than the closer stars. That means, the farther the star is, the faster it is moving out.

This prompted scientists to guess that the whole Universe was expanding!

Was that difficult to understand?

Ok, now take a plastic sheet. Mark two points on the sheet. Move the sheet as a whole away from you. The distance between the two points will remain the same. This movement is simply a geometric displacement of the entire sheet. Now, instead of moving the sheet as it is, hold one side of the sheet and pull the other end of the sheet, thereby stretching it.

Now, the distance between the two marked points will increase. If we observe the sheet ourselves, the distant point will appear to move much faster from us than the closer point.

This is what is happening to our Universe. Our Universe is expanding!

Go to any room in your house. Release a coloured gaseous substance in the centre of the room so that you can observe it. You will notice that the coloured gas slowly spreads and occupies a large part of the room. This is also expansion.

But the expansion of the Universe we are talking about is not the same. It is not that there is a well defined region in the space, fixed perfectly and that the Universe containing matter is expanding within that.

The Universe is the collection of *all* matter. And this collection of matter is expanding. The matter remains more or less the same. Just that the blank space between different chunks of matter is increasing as the Universe is expanding.

Our own Solar system is moving away from the centre of the Milky Way galaxy. The Milky Way galaxy is moving away from the Andromeda galaxy. All galaxies are moving away from one another.

The boundaries of the Universe constantly stretch, and thus what we consider space is constantly expanding.

Newtonian collapse!

The idea that the Universe is expanding is very important. Because, if this is not the case, the physical models of the Universe will be very unstable.

Newton had proposed that objects are attracted to each other. If this was the only force operating, the entire Universe would be collapsing into one point. Any two stars will start attracting each other and they will collapse into a single being. With this as a starting point, all stars and planets will collapse into this mass and so on.

Why is this not happening?

Newton's claim of bodies attracting each other has been proven to be correct. The only reason the bodies have not collapsed into one single mass is that they are constantly and slowly moving out. The pace of the movement is very small–spread over several million years.

From this we can conclude that, at some point in time in the very distant past, all the stars were much closer to one another than they are now.

We will examine this aspect in a later chapter.

*

Let us stop at this point, since we will be revisiting this after a short break. During this break, let us take a look at what this whole Universe is made of.

What is the Universe made of?

By now, we have more questions than answers. Who created the Sun, its planets including our own Earth, the various moons, all the other pieces in our galaxy and the rest of the Universe?

What is the composition of each of the planets and stars? What is the difference between stars and planets? Are all planets alike? If so, is life possible in all the planets?

Who placed each of the planets where they are? Who started their motion? What is keeping them in motion? Are they likely to change their paths? Are they likely to leave a particular orbit and move away? Will they slow down?

How many elements are there?

Let us take up just one question in this chapter, that of the composition of the various pieces in the Universe.

Let us start with our Earth. Our ancestors believed that all the objects on the Earth were made of five fundamental elements: water, fire, air, Earth and sky. The Greeks thought so, the Indians thought so too.

But modern science tells us that these five elements are not really fundamental elements. In fact one of them–the sky–is nothing but a visual effect. The other–fire–is a process, one or more chemical substances mixing with oxygen and reacting chemically. During the burning process, several different visual effects are seen. The flame created is in different colours. There may or may not be smoke.

Air is a mixture of several elements and compounds. Water is a compound made of two fundamental elements. Earth, or a piece of mud or sand, is again a mixture of several elements and compounds.

Now we are moving very fast. Let's pause and think a little. What are elements and compounds? Let us look at them in detail.

Elements and compounds

Over the centuries, humans could isolate and extract several metals from the Earth, most notably iron, gold, silver, aluminium and copper. Metals were shining, hard and strong. Yet, they were soft and easy to work with when heated. Metals could be melted and mixed in various proportions to create alloys (such as bronze and steel).

Humans had also succeeded in extracting several non-metals such as carbon and sulphur.

All these metals and non-metals reacted with one another and the air, when mixed and heated. They resulted in various new substances. Several of these substances created by such reactions were also found naturally on the surface of the Earth.

All these substances were known as inorganic substances. They were extracted from the lifeless part of the Earth.

Humans also obtained several plant extracts and animal extracts. Such chemicals were called organic substances–meaning, they were extracted from life forms.

The practical method of mixing the above substances and creating new substances is called Chemistry. For centuries, people practised this science, without a proper understanding of the chemicals involved.

It was only in the 19th century that scientists began understanding the fundamental building blocks of all the things they were seeing on the Earth.

They identified a bunch of basic substances which could not be created by chemical reactions involving other substances. These basic substances were named elements.

By the year 1800, 25 such elements had been discovered. By 1869, 60 elements were discovered. The Russian scientist **Dmitri Mendeleev** organised these 60 elements into what he called a Periodic Table. By 1900, 80 elements had been discovered. Within a decade, 92 elements were discovered.

These 92 are available naturally on the surface of the Earth. We can confirm as of today that no other element occurs naturally. However, several more have been synthesised since then, through nuclear fusion. As of today, we have a total of 117 elements including 25 created in the laboratory.

The composition of an atom

Greek philosophers thought about the building blocks of objects. They thought if you keep splitting any object into two, and further sub-divide one of the pieces into two, and keep repeating this process, you end up with a very small piece. This piece cannot be further sub-divided. They named such an indivisible piece as an atom.

We use the same concept. To understand an element, you have to understand what the element itself is composed of. If we consider an element a fundamental substance–something which cannot be created by combining other substances–an atom is its basic unit. If the element is a wall, the atom is the brick with which the wall has been built.

In the early part of the 20th century, a series of discoveries made possible a better understanding of the structure of the atom. **J J Thomson** discovered a new object as an isolated particle while experimenting in electricity. He named it an electron. He quickly pointed out that every element (discovered until then) must have electrons in it.

In 1918, Ernest **Rutherford**, a New Zealander living in Britain separated a proton. He also predicted in 1920, the possibility of another sub-atomic particle, which he named the neutron. But it took another British scientist

James Chadwick a tough search over a period of ten years to locate the neutron.

With this, the structure of the atom was complete. Each atom was made of a certain number of protons and electrons. The number of protons and electrons was exactly the same in each atom of a particular element, and this number was known as the atomic number of the element. In each element the number of neutrons came close to the number of protons but didn't have to match exactly.

Particles	Mass (kg)	Diameter (m)
Electron	9.1094×10^{-31}	$<10^{-18}$
Proton	1.6726×10^{-27}	10^{-15}
Neutron	1.6749×10^{-27}	10^{-13}

The proton and the electron matched each other on the value of the electric charge held in them, but they were of opposite directions. The electron had a negative charge and the proton a positive charge. The neutron, on the other hand, was neutral (hence the name). The proton and neutron weighed close enough, but an electron was extremely light when compared to a proton or a neutron.

The most interesting thing was that every element (discovered until then and thereafter) contained identical looking electrons, protons and neutrons. Thus, it can be said that the most fundamental things in the Earth are these three particles—electrons, protons and neutrons.

The lightest and simplest element was Hydrogen. It had only one proton, one electron and no neutron. The next element, Helium had two protons, two neutrons and two electrons. Thereafter, you could increase the number of protons by one, balance the same with an increase in the electron count, add appropriate number of neutrons and you had a new element.

That is how we have now reached till 118, of which the element with the atomic number 117 has not yet been created. It may be possible that in future more elements may be created artificially. Other than the 92 elements that occur naturally on the Earth's surface, the rest are unnatural—that is, they quickly change themselves into other elements within a short period of time.

Chemical reactions

Scientists observed and analysed numerous chemical substances found on the Earth, and discovered that they were various combinations of these basic elements. The water we drink everyday is made up of Hydrogen and Oxygen in a certain proportion.

It is not as if you take these two elements Hydrogen and Oxygen and shake them vigorously to produce water. You have to make them chemically react by bringing the atoms of both close enough. One way this can be done is by heating the mixture of the two gases. The result is water, which is stable by itself. It can't be converted back into Hydrogen and Oxygen just like that. You have to apply an electric current through the water to break it into Hydrogen and Oxygen.

The same is true of common salt, called Sodium Chloride. It is a combination of the Sodium metal and Chlorine gas. But here, the reaction is spontaneous. You just have to bring Sodium and Chlorine together, and immediately they react, to create common salt.

Just as an atom is the basic block for an element, for compounds it is the molecule. Thus, one molecule of water consists of two atoms of Hydrogen and one atom of Oxygen, strongly bonded to each other. In the case of Sodium Chloride, each molecule consists of an atom of Sodium and an atom of Chlorine. The binding force between these atoms within a molecule is quite strong, and takes a fair bit of effort to break up.

Elements and compounds exist in three different states—solid, liquid and gas. Every element and compound changes its state, when heated or cooled. When you take water and cool it below zero degree centigrade (0°C), it becomes solid ice. When the same water is taken and boiled to 100 degrees centigrade, it becomes water vapour—a gaseous substance.

The same is true for Oxygen or Hydrogen or a metal like say Iron or Gold. Oxygen, which in its natural form is a gas, can be cooled to liquid (at minus 183 degree centigrade) and then cooled further to solid (at minus 219 degree centigrade). Iron, which in its natural form is a solid, can be heated so that it melts into a liquid (at 1538 degree centigrade) and then upon further heating can become a gas (at 2861 degree centigrade).

Scientists did detailed analysis of numerous objects on Earth, including living and non-living matter. They found that our human bodies, bodies of animals and plants were made of the same few elements, but in slightly differing proportions. The Earth's crust, the substances under the Earth's surface, the air above us—

all were made of the same elements or compounds made of these elements.

Thus, we can conclude that the whole Earth is made of fundamental elements. These elements in turn are made of the three sub-atomic particles–protons, neutrons and electrons.

Just when we thought we had a clear idea of the making of the Earth, there were more amazing discoveries.

Anti-matter

In 1928, **Paul Dirac**, a British scientist came up with a theory that showed that for every charged particle, there should also be a particle with an opposite charge but the same weight. Thus, he predicted that there should be an anti-electron, a particle with the same mass as that of the electron but with a positive charge.

In 1932, **Carl Anderson** observed precisely such a particle. This particle was identical to an electron except for its positive charge. This particle was named the positron.

If this indeed was true, there should also be an anti-proton, the exact opposite of a proton.

However, finding the anti-proton took a longer time. **Owen Chamberlain,** an American physicist, discovered this particle in 1955.

Though these anti-particles have been identified, they are not observed in large numbers, as much as electrons or protons, in our world.

What will happen if an electron and a positron meet? They will be attracted to each other, bang into each other and both will be destroyed to become a burst of energy.

This made scientists come up with theories on how electrons and positrons would have come into being in the first place. It might have been that a burst of light energy suddenly split into two particles—one electron and one positron.

But let us not jump further. We will revisit this at a later time.

Let us just be happy for now that there are very few positrons and anti-protons in the world that we live in. Otherwise all of us will vanish into bursts of energy!

So, as far as we are concerned, the fundamental particles are the electron, proton and neutron. They combine to form several unique elements. These elements react in various ways amongst themselves and create compounds.

These elements and compounds together have made what we ourselves are and other life forms including plants and animals.

What are stars and other planets made of?

Now, this is Earth. What about other planets? The Sun? Other stars?

Are they made up of the same elements we have on the Earth? Are they likely to have something more? Anything new?

Human beings have directly visited only one other celestial body. The Moon.

The Americans and Russians have sent spacecraft to the surface of the Moon, from where samples have been brought back to the Earth. The Americans have also landed on the Moon.

Pilot-less crafts have been sent by the Russians, the Americans, the European Space Agency and the Japanese to planets such as Mars, Venus, Jupiter and Mercury.

Mars and Venus are the planets closest to the Earth. Landing crafts have landed on the surface of these planets and measured the temperature and pressure on their surfaces. Photographs have been taken of the planets.

We have a lot more to learn about Mars and Venus. We have even more to learn about the other planets. We simply cannot send any spacecraft to the Sun–the craft will be burnt even before it reaches the surface of the Sun.

From what little we know, we can say that the elements on Earth also exist in other planets, but a lot of what is found on the Earth's surface is not available in some of the other planets. Water may not exist in any of the other planets.

The stars are a different story altogether.

Unlike the planets, a star is a happening place.

Before understanding what is happening inside the stars, we need to understand what plasma is.

Similar to the three states of matter–gas, liquid, solid– plasma is considered yet another state, all by itself, and distinct from the other three states. In a gas, liquid or solid matter, each atom retains all its electrons and protons intact. There may be an odd atom here or there which may have lost an electron or two.

But, in plasma, negatively charged electrons from most of the atoms will be roaming freely. Correspondingly, the rest of each atom will be positively charged, and they will also be roaming freely. We call this 'positively charged rest of the atom' an ion.

Thus, in plasma, there are free ions and free electrons, all mixed up in a kind of soup. The soup is at a very high temperature and pressure where the atoms keep hitting each other and the resulting collision keeps knocking off the electrons from the atoms.

Stars contain such plasma.

Our Sun contains in its core, the plasma of Hydrogen and Helium. For the Sun, 74% by mass is Hydrogen (Atomic number = 1) and 25% by mass is Helium (Atomic number = 2).

The Sun must have started only with Hydrogen. Because of the massive heat at the core of the Sun, nuclear fusion happens resulting in the formation of Helium. Four Hydrogen atoms come close—they contain four protons and four electrons. Under the heat, they fuse to create a single Helium atom containing two protons, two neutrons and two electrons. Some mass is lost in the process, but a lot of heat and light is created during this process.

Since this fusion creates more heat, this aids fusion even more.

Once a substantial portion of Hydrogen is converted to Helium, further nuclear fusion will convert Helium to Lithium. Then, further nuclear fusion will generate Beryllium, Boron, Carbon and so on–all elements with higher and higher atomic numbers.

Now you can guess what might have happened in the planets. Planets were also once hot stars or part of hot stars, and contained only Hydrogen plasma to start with. Then, through nuclear fusion, all kinds of higher elements were produced. Eventually, when the nuclear fusion could not be sustained any more, the whole star started cooling down.

Planets might have come into being when a small piece of a star got thrown off, and it started circling the mother star. It also went through the cycle of nuclear fission, creating several higher elements. In due course, the nuclear reactions stopped and they cooled down to become solid matter.

That is why we have all kinds of elements on the surface of the Earth but almost nothing more than Hydrogen and Helium in the Sun.

All the stars we see (including our Sun) are large plasma balls containing mostly Hydrogen and Helium, performing nuclear fusion every second and releasing large amounts of energy in the form of light and heat. That is why we are able to see them. There is more to stars and we will revisit them later.

Stars including our Sun also have some elements with higher atomic numbers (a very small percentage–The Sun has these elements less than 1% by mass). These elements might have been formed in an earlier star and reached the current star.

Planets, on the other hand, are cool places. They may have a 'hot core' still. The Earth's core has very hot lava. This is what erupts from volcanoes. Some planets which are far from the Sun may not have a hot core.

We will come back to the stars, the planets and other celestial objects later. Before that, let us take a look at how small particles move, what governs their motion, etc.

The mechanics of small particles

We have seen how large objects move. The planets circle the Sun at a rapid speed. The Earth spins around its axis quite fast. The distances between the objects in the planetary system are large.

Newton came up with equations which explained this motion quite well. Will the same set of rules apply to small particles? These particles–electrons, protons, neutrons, atoms, molecules–are extremely small in size. The distances between these particles within an atom are just as small.

What are the laws governing their motion?

The structure of an atom

Before Rutherford's time, the prevailing model of the atom was called Dalton's model. This model assumed that the atom looks like a pudding of positively charged matter. In this matter, negatively charged electrons are embedded like plums in a pudding.

If this is the case, if you take a gold foil (you could as well take any other metal or non-metal), and shoot alpha particles, they will be blocked by the pudding.

If you throw a tennis ball at a wall, what would you expect? You expect the wall to bounce the tennis ball back to you.

But when Rutherford shot the alpha particles at the gold foil, most of the alpha particles simply went through and reached the other side. Only an odd alpha particle here and there bounced back.

This experiment was repeated with other metals, and with foils of different thicknesses. The result was the same.

This was possible only if much of the atom was empty space, through which the alpha particle simply sailed through. Only at the small core of an atom, must all the protons and neutrons be sitting. The electrons cannot be part of this core since they are of a different charge. They must be at a distance from the core. They are also likely to be orbiting the core for stability.

The core of the atom is called the nucleus.

This model is known as Rutherford's model of the atom, and has since been improved substantially.

An alpha particle is the nucleus of the Helium atom. We know that the Helium nucleus consists of two protons and two neutrons, and is quite small. The Gold atom on the other hand consists of 79 protons and 118 neutrons.

Taking Rutherford's model of the atom, we can conclude that much of what looks like the solid walls in our houses is full of large, gaping holes. Electrons, protons and neutrons can simply flow across our walls without any interruption whatsoever.

This is like a piece of cloth. If you look through closely, you will find threads straight and across. A solid object cannot go through this, but water can seep through this cloth.

Isotopes

We saw earlier that for a given element, the number of protons and electrons should be identical, and that the number of neutrons will be close enough to that of protons but need not be equal. For the same element, a few variations occur in the number of neutrons. Each such variation is called an isotope.

For example, we have seen that Hydrogen normally has one proton, one electron and no neutron. This is known as Protium. There is a variant which contains one proton, one electron and one neutron. This naturally occurring variant is called Deuterium. Likewise, another variant called Tritium exists, containing two neutrons. Of the Hydrogen naturally available in the Earth, only 0.0025% at most–that is one in 40,000–is Deuterium. Tritium is even less.

Several elements have isotopes. These isotopes are important when it comes to nuclear fusion, which we will see later.

From small to big

Now, we can reasonably understand what seems to have happened. A whole bunch of minute sub-atomic particles have combined to form a series of fundamental elements, and they in turn–somehow–have shaped various objects in the Universe–the Sun, the planets, their moons, the galaxies and so on.

Energy, light and gravity

We have seen the big, we have seen the small. But there are a few more important things we have to understand, before we can piece together how our Universe might have started and reached where it is.

Our understanding so far has been about matter. That is, objects which occupy space and contain mass. Their weight can be measured. They may have positive or negative electric charge. They may have magnetic properties.

There is another key aspect–energy.

Energy is of several types. When an object moves, it is supposed to have kinetic energy. When chemical substances burn they release chemical energy inherent in them, in the form of heat. The heat energy in turn can be used to create light. Heat energy is also used and converted into mechanical (kinetic energy) through devices such as steam engines.

Our ancestors understood energy very well. They invented fire a long time ago and used it effectively to produce heat to cook their food, and for light.

Until electric current was generated and used effectively in the 19th century, fire was the source of light, whether from oil lamps or candles.

Thermodynamics

The study of heat energy and the changes in temperature and pressure of a closed system containing particles resulted in the field known as Thermodynamics.

As a result of this study, scientists came to the conclusion that energy cannot be created or destroyed. It can only be converted from one form to another. This is known as the principle of conservation of energy.

If you take a piece of wood and burn it, the wood merely releases the energy inside it into heat. This heat is not coming from anywhere outside. It is within the wood.

Thermodynamics also helped understand a concept called entropy. Entropy is the state of order in a system.

My table in my office is very disorderly. When I moved into my office room, it was quite ordered. There was nothing on my table! But everyday I added something more to my table. After a few days the table looked so cluttered.

At times, I am extremely annoyed and clear the entire table–that is, I mostly throw out things. But then within the next few days, the table goes back to its chaotic state.

When you start with a very orderly table, the entropy is considered to be low. With every piece of junk thrown on top of the table, the entropy keeps increasing.

Thermodynamics tells us that in general, entropy of the Universe is constantly increasing. That is, what was once quite orderly is now constantly moving towards chaos. Just like my table.

Light

We are creatures of light. If not for sunlight, there may not have been any life on our planet.

We understand that light is a form of energy. When you heat up some objects, they start emitting light.

It was Newton–once again–who understood that white light is not truly a single chunk. Through a prism, he split the white light into its components–VIBGYOR–Violet, Indigo, Blue, Green, Yellow, Orange and Red. Yes, the colours of the rainbow!

Newton thought of light as particles. But subsequent theorists disagreed. A Dutch mathematician, **Christiaan Huygens** proposed that light is some kind of a wave.

There is a classical experiment called Young's double slit experiment. A single slit is made in an opaque sheet. Next to that yet another sheet, with two slits at equal distance above and below the slit in the first sheet, is placed. When light is beamed through the first sheet, it goes through the slit, and then through the next two slits resulting in a pattern of light and dark fringes on the screen at a distance.

From this, scientists concluded that light must be spreading like a wave from a light source.

Particle, wave duality of light

Albert Einstein, the greatest scientist since Isaac Newton, came up with a series of research papers which changed physics forever.

Young's double slit experiment

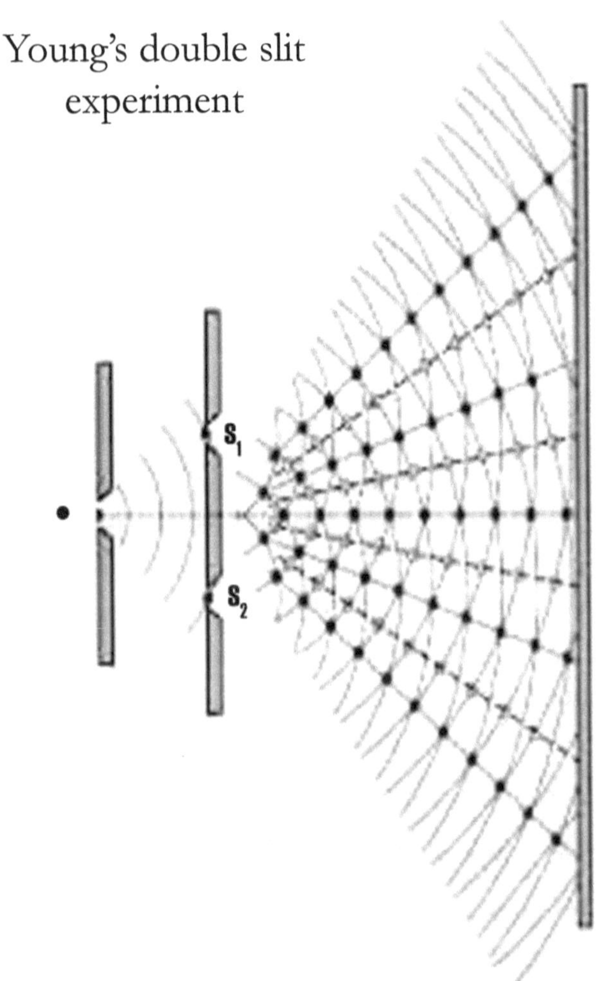

Einstein was studying the impact of light falling on certain material. In this material, when light fell on the surface, electrons on the surface were expelled. Such materials are called photoelectric.

When the intensity of a given light falling on the surface increased, this did not result in increased velocity of the electrons. Instead, more electrons were displaced, but with the same velocity as before.

On the other hand, when light of a higher frequency fell on the surface, the displaced electrons were at a higher velocity.

This led Einstein to conclude that the light was in the form of photons or quanta of energy.

This revolutionary understanding meant that light behaved like a wave, and it also behaved like packets, or almost like particles.

This concept is called duality of light.

Duality of particles

Just as light energy exhibits a dual nature, interesting experiments have revealed duality of particles.

Particles are matter with well defined mass and they occupy specific volume.

The electron is a well defined particle that we saw before.

When electrons were used in a Young double slit experiment structure instead of light, the result was an identical fringe pattern. This was possible only if a stream of electrons behaved exactly like a ray of light.

This was an equally revolutionary breakthrough in understanding our universe.

Light behaves like particles. Particles behave like light.

Light has a maximum speed of 300,000 kilometres per second. All known particles travel at a speed slower than that.

Light does not have any mass. All particles have some mass, however small they may be.

Energy - mass relationship

In the same year Einstein explained the photoelectric phenomenon which fetched him a Nobel Prize, he also proposed his Special Theory of Relativity. As part of his calculations, he came up with an equation that linked energy, mass and the speed of light.

This equation has been made famous on T-shirts these days: $E = mc^2$. Here, 'm' refers to the mass of any stationary object, 'c', the velocity of light and 'E', the energy inherent in that object.

In Thermodynamics, we have seen the law of conservation of energy. After Einstein's famous equation, we now have to talk about the law of conservation of energy and mass.

Even though energy cannot be created out of thin air, it can be created by destroying some mass. This is exactly what happens in either nuclear fission or nuclear fusion.

If a nucleus of an unstable heavy element such as Uranium is attacked with a fast moving particle like alpha particle (nucleus of a Helium atom) or a neutron, in the resultant melee, the unstable atom splits and becomes a couple of lesser atoms (atoms of elements with lower atomic numbers).

Henri Becquerel, a French scientist observed naturally occurring Uranium releasing spontaneous radiation. **Marie Curie** and her husband **Pierre Curie** discovered more naturally radioactive elements such as Polonium and Radium.

During the Second World War, scientists in the United States of America worked together to perfect nuclear fission facilitating the breaking up of Uranium atoms as a chain reaction, by bombarding them with neutrons. The result was the most destructive weapon the world has ever seen–the atom bomb.

Atom bombs were dropped on Japan by America, not once, but twice, with devastating effect. The destroyed mass, less than a few grams, released large quantities of destructive energy in which entire cities were destroyed and millions of people killed.

Since then, though advanced versions of these nuclear devices have been created, so far no war time explosions have happened. Instead, nuclear energy has been put to good use by converting controlled nuclear fission into electrical energy.

We have already seen that nuclear fusion happens in the Sun and other stars generating energy. So far, humans have not been able to manage a similar effect on Earth in a controlled manner to generate energy.

Relativity, Time and speed of light

When Newton put together his concepts of motion, one of the vital basis on which his entire theory stood was that of an absolute time. All of us have a sense of time.

We believe and feel that time passes by, whether we perform an action or sit still or sleep. We have heard the famous saying: 'Time and tide wait for no man'.

We also know that passage of time is the same for all of us. If five seconds are over in my watch, then your watch should also show the same.

In other words, our intuition tells us that time as a concept is independent of other physical phenomena.

But, our intuition can be wrong. Several great minds have been fooled by such intuition. Einstein was not fooled.

We call two events to be simultaneous if they happen at the 'same time'. How do we know that events are happening at the same time?

This can only be done if we keep monitoring the events with clocks which are synchronised with each other and one clock sends signals to the other clock every time an event takes place.

Suppose these signals are sent in the form of light and we know the distance between the events well before, we can find out when an event is happening at a far away place, sitting where we are, by just monitoring the signals.

Newtonian mechanics indicated that speed of an object appears differently to a stationary observer and an observer who is moving along with the object. If you travel in a train, to you the person sitting in front of you seems to remain stationary. But to a person standing on the platform where the train is whizzing past, the person sitting in the seat is moving.

But, it has been observed through experiments that the speed of light is constant even if the light source is moving, either towards us or away from us.

Thus it was observed that the speed of the light is a fundamental property, which is constant and unchanging. If this was the case, for an observer who is stationary and another observer who is moving–sitting on top of a light source, something else must be changing, if the laws of mechanics have to remain true.

Einstein used this concept and arrived at a shocking conclusion.

Time is not absolute.

If an observer is sitting on top of a moving body which is moving quite fast–at a speed comparable to that of the speed of light–he would feel that the passage of time is a bit slow, compared to a stationary observer.

Let us explain this further. Take two clocks. Synchronise them so that they show the same time. Keep one stationary on Earth. Put the other in a spacecraft and send it on a high speed journey to the Moon or a faraway planet and then bring it back. Now compare the time in the two clocks. The clock that had journeyed in the rocket would show less than the clock which is stationary.

Not easy to believe?

This was the conclusion drawn by Einstein from his Special Theory of Relativity.

This is also posed as the 'Twin Paradox'. Take two twin sisters. Put one of them in a high speed rocket and send her on a journey to all the planets. She finally arrives back after several years. The one on the Earth will not exactly be stationary! She will be moving around, but will not be undertaking a high speed journey like her sister! When the rocket sister arrives all young and 18, she will find her twin, an old lady of probably 55!

Is this really possible? No one has tried it, but the theory says so. However clocks have been sent up in high speed rockets and have been observed to show a slower passage of time.

Though our intuition says something else, we have to accept that time is not absolute and can shrink related to the speed at which one travels.

Bending of light

Einstein was set to shock the world anyway, so why stop with time alone?

All of us have observed a light beam. We see the light travelling in a perfectly straight line.

You have to expect Einstein not to believe this.

Einstein said not just the objects with mass are attracted by heavy objects due to gravity, but light also is attracted to heavy bodies. So, light curves near heavy bodies.

That is, light is not travelling in a straight line in the sense of what we see as straight.

Einstein was mostly a theoretician. He kept exploring with his mind and came up with such predictions. Now, it is the job of scientists to prove him right or wrong.

Einstein reported his finding (General Theory of Relativity) well before the First World War. **Arthur Eddington**, an English astrophysicist, set out to experimentally verify whether light indeed bends near heavy objects. But with the onset of the war in Europe, Eddington could not travel to verify this fact and did so only after the war was over.

The heaviest object near where we live happens to be the Sun. When the Sun is bright, its brightness makes it difficult for us to view other stars behind the Sun and at a longer distance from us than the Sun.

But on the day of an eclipse, when the Sun is blocked by the Moon coming between the Sun and the Earth, we should be able to see the stars farther than the Sun. Though the Sun has been blocked by the Moon, the Sun is still very much there. Therefore, if Einstein is right, the light from the stars beyond the Sun should be curved when they reach the Earth.

Eddington travelled to the island of Principe in Africa, monitored the Solar Eclipse on 29th May 1919 and took pictures of the eclipse and other stars in the region beyond the Sun. His results proved Einstein's theory of gravity to be correct.

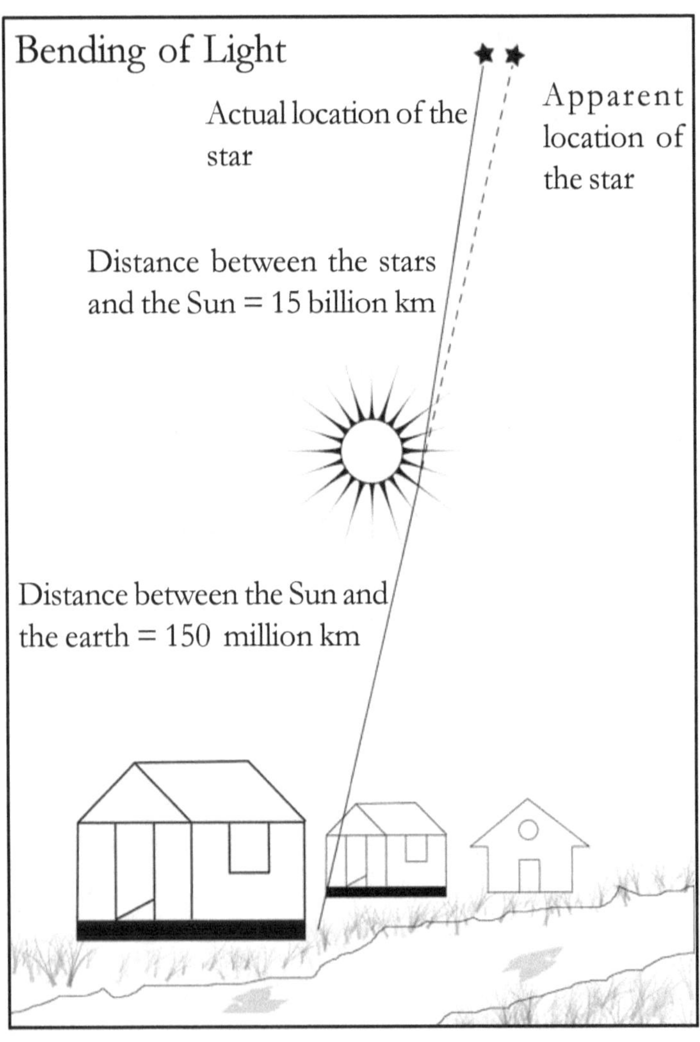

Bending of Light
Actual location of the star
Apparent location of the star
Distance between the stars and the Sun = 15 billion km
Distance between the Sun and the earth = 150 million km

Black holes and others

We already saw in the previous chapter what was happening inside stars. Now we are revisiting that area, with a better understanding of Einstein's theory of gravitation and also the behaviour of light.

We saw that stars are made of Hydrogen plasma. Inside stars, violent nuclear fusion is taking place causing Hydrogen to become Helium and generating heat and light.

In addition, the gravitational effect will be pulling all the plasma elements–free ions and free electrons making them come closer and closer. Gravity will be bringing the plasma closer while the pressure building inside will be pushing the matter out as long as nuclear fusion is taking place.

What happens when the star runs out of fuel?

This was an interesting problem thought of by an Indian Physics student **Subrahmanyan Chandrasekhar**, on voyage by ship from India to Cambridge University in England. While on the ship, he came to the conclusion that if the star starts with a mass below 1.44 times that of our Sun, then after it runs out of fuel, it will settle down to an object called the White Dwarf.

It is called a Dwarf because it has a mass as large as the Sun, but has a size only as large as that of the Earth. It is called White because though it does not generate any more heat and light–its nuclear fusion has stopped–it is still hot and hence it emits radiation. Eventually, it will cool down and become what is known as a Black Dwarf– it won't emit much light anymore.

What will happen to the stars that start with a mass more than the Chandrasekhar limit? That is, when the mass is more than 1.44 times that of the Sun?

Since it is a massive star, it starts burning very fast and loses all its fuel much faster than the smaller stars. Once the burning is complete, it cannot sustain itself because it is so huge and the gravitational pull shrinks it substantially. It contains mainly neutrons.

Because of the massive gravitational pull, the protons and electrons come together and combine to form a neutron. This process is known as electron capture. This is how, what originally started as a star containing Hydrogen ions and electrons, eventually becomes an object full of neutrons. Because of this, it is called a Neutron Star.

The Universe

A Neutron Star generally has a mass two or three times that of the Sun, but a radius which is the size of Tirupati! Just imagine taking two Suns and shrinking them into a sphere the size of Tirupati! Neutron stars are extremely dense.

What if the massive star starts with an original mass five times or more than that of our Sun?

It will burn even faster than above and once the burning is over, it will start collapsing into itself.

Since it is so massive, the collapse will be so much, the mass of about five Suns will be shrunk into the size of your palm!

The resultant body is known as a black hole.

It is called a black hole because it cannot be observed at all. The reason is that it has such a massive gravitational force, any light wave coming past that body will get sucked into that body and will never escape.

It was Einstein's gravitational theory that predicted the presence of such objects and it has subsequently been proved right.

Any object thrown close to the black hole will get sucked in and destroyed inside the black hole.

Huge stars, before becoming black holes would have exploded in a burst. Such a process is known as Super Nova explosion.

During this period, a Super Nova emits as much radiation in a few weeks as done by our Sun over a period of 10 billion years!

Chinese astronomers as early as the 2nd century AD seem to have observed super nova explosion. In our galaxy, a super nova explosion happens once in 50 years.

*

Great. We now know quite a bit about physical phenomena, celestial bodies, fundamental particles and so on. Let us now try to understand how our Universe that we see today might have come about.

Big Bang Theory

We saw that the Universe is expanding. That means, at some point earlier, the stars and other celestial objects must have been close enough to each other.

Keep going back in time. You may reach a time when the entire matter in the Universe must have been together as a single ball of plasma. It has been estimated that this is about 13.7 billion years.

The big bang theory proposes the following model for the birth of the Universe that we see today.

At the beginning of the present Universe, the entire matter in the form of plasma was crushed into a very small space. Under heavy gravity of the mass, it had reached a stage where the pressure was just too much to handle.

This resulted in a massive explosion and expansion.

During the early period immediately after the big bang explosion, there were plenty of chaotic processes, eventually ending in the presence of electrons and protons and a lot of energy in the form of photons.

The matter so created (electrons and protons) slowly started moving around. Stars in which protons (Hydrogen ions) started combining together to become Helium ions and so on were formed.

The scattering of matter was not entirely uniform. In some places more dense matter settled. Elsewhere, the density was low. This resulted in the formation of galaxies as we see today. At the centre of the galaxy, massive black holes are present. Elsewhere in the galaxy, we see burning stars, cooled down planets, etc.

Our Sun is estimated to be 4.57 billion years old. Our Earth was also born around the same time.

The Universe, since the big bang, has been expanding to this day. This process will keep happening, but may stop at a future time. When the expansion stops, Newton's theory on gravitational attraction will take over and the Universe will start shrinking.

When this shrinking continues, eventually the whole Universe may reach the size of your palm! This is called the Big Crunch–the opposite of the Big Bang.

Once again, at this point, another big bang will happen, yet another Universe will be created and this process may keep happening forever.

We are merely living in one instance of the Universe. The earlier instances may not have looked exactly like what we see today. In a previous instance (or in the next instance), there may not be an Earth, there may not be any life form, or may be, there will be…

The universal constants as we see now, such as the speed of light or the Planck's constant, could be different. The fundamental elements may be different. The electron may look different, may have a different charge, may have a different mass.

Time and space will be unique to each instance of the universe. At the time of the big crunch and the following big bang, nothing can be carried over as everything will be destroyed. Such a point is known as a singularity.

This whole destruction and re-creation of the universe may have happened several times over, with no specific origin and ending.

Does this sound like the Vedic philosophical model of pralaya and creation of the universe after that period?

This is the most widely accepted model of the universe as of today.

Our understanding may change if new facts emerge.

*

It is a fantastic feeling to know that today we have been able to unravel some of the mysteries of the Universe which had bothered our ancestors for so long.

But we now have just as many new questions to answer—like how life forms evolved in this Universe and that too why only in our Earth. There are so many other questions that require answers as well.

What the great scientists before us have tried to do is to look seriously for the answers.

If we too continue to look for answers to such questions, the knowledge we gather is sure to enrich our lives. Maybe you will become a Newton or an Einstein when you grow up and come up with some answers like them!

***